# Antenna Country

# Antenna Country

*by*

**Kay Landers**

Chicago ● Moody Press

ISBN: 0-8024-0245-3

*Printed in the United States of America*

*To each missionary who has ever served with HCJB. You are the ones who have made possible forty years of mission history.*

"Missionary radio? . . . It works, it opens the doors, it opens the mind, it opens the hearts. When the Word of God comes in, the promise is, 'The entrance of thy Word giveth light.' That's all we're in Ecuador for, not trying to change people's religion. We long ago learned that there wasn't any use wasting five minutes trying to change a man's religion. But if need be, we would give our lives to see them become new creatures in Christ. Radio is just a vehicle, a wagon to deliver the cargo, the precious cargo of God's Word . . . we don't worship radio, but we thank God for His Word which produces results which have been seen in thousands and thousands of lives . . . ."

DR. C. W. JONES

# PREFACE

This is a true story. Every event in this book actually took place. But in telling the story of HCJB I was confronted with a problem — the missionary. How could I include everyone? I couldn't. Too many people have made their contributions to the work of the pioneer missionary broadcaster. My only solution was to present the missionary as a composite drawing, and this is what I have attempted to do.

It would be impossible though to leave out the three men who have directed the mission. HCJB was the dream of Dr. and Mrs. Clarence Jones and Dr. and Mrs. Reuben Larson. The Larsons were already missionaries in Ecuador when the two men met in 1929 in the United States. Dr. Jones then canvassed countries of South America. The Republic of Ecuador invited him to set up a radio station in Quito. Dr. Larson knew Ecuador; Dr. Jones knew radio. For many years both families lived in Quito. The cofounders and their wives are still living, and to them goes grateful acknowledgment for their faithfulness to the vision God gave them.

Since 1962, Dr. Abe Van Der Puy has been president of HCJB. Dr. Van Der Puy and his wife Dolores (who died in 1965) came to Ecuador in 1945, and for many years he served in various aspects of the Ecuadorian ministry. Today, lovingly supported by his wife Marj, he provides vigorous and intelligent leadership to all facets of the mission organization.

HCJB are the call letters for the long- and short-wave facilities in Quito, Ecuador. They have also become the name by which most people know The World Radio Missionary Fellowship, Inc., and for this reason I always refer to the mission as HCJB.

A sister station to HCJB operates in Panama City under the call letters HOXO. This station is twenty-one years old and has a 5,000-watt AM voice which broadcasts eighteen hours daily in both Spanish and English.

I want to thank Nancy Woolnough for giving me the impression that it was possible for me to complete this assignment. Mary Skinner and Dick Broach provided me with the needed psychological boosts, and I am grateful to them. Lynne Lind typed the manuscript and Joe Springer read it, and I appreciate the time they invested in this project. Imogene Booker released me from other responsibilities, and her consideration of the work schedule deserves a word of thanks. I am also very pleased that Yvonne McGuire shared with me in this book by doing the favorable sketches.

I used the paraphrase of 1 Corinthians 13 from a World Day of Prayer program, and I acknowledge John Gunther's *Inside Latin America* as a source book. My husband and three children are thankful that "the book" is now completed.

# CONTENTS

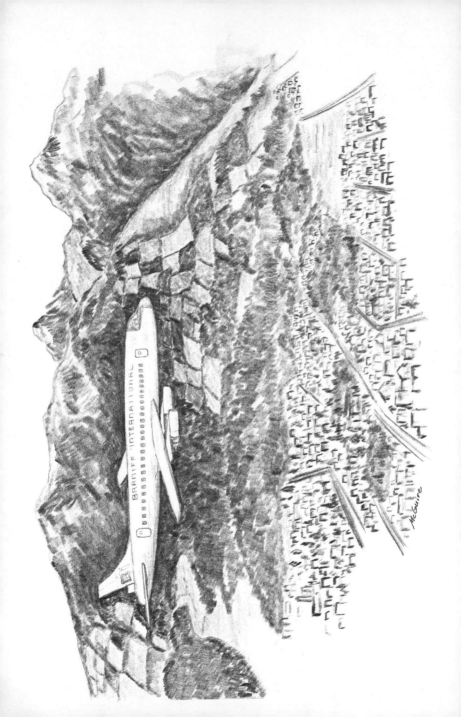

# 1

# Return to Quito

The bright orange jet lifted easily off the wet Panamanian airstrip. Within minutes the "No Smoking" sign was switched off, and the thirteen young children scattered among the one hundred adults watched for the seat-belt sign to darken so they could be released from their confinement.

Hours earlier, the flight had left Miami in the dark night, a tropical storm enclosing the plane on takeoff. But the massive engines had rapidly taken the colorful jet above the disturbance. When the pilot announced that the island of Cuba was "right below," the passengers could see only a huge covering of black clouds beneath them and a thousand stars above.

Most of the people had slept from Miami to Panama. But after they had left the Central American republic behind, the sun gave everyone a sense of a new day. Businessmen ran tired fingers over their stubbled chins and wondered if they needed to shave. Children teased accommodating parents to give up their window seats.

A group of six exchange students from New Jersey took out their Spanish dictionaries and began quizzing each other on subjunctive verbs. Across the aisle a Peruvian family showed no outward sign that they heard the harsh pronunciation.

A long line formed in front of the rest rooms. People began to think in terms of hot coffee as the stewardess expertly shuttled breakfast trays onto the counter. Everyone seemed occupied — everyone except Jon.

Jon had remained immobile the entire trip. Only once, shortly after leaving Florida, had he moved, and then just to push his seat backward so that his long slender legs wouldn't be cramped. Stretched out comfortably, he slept. He hadn't bothered to leave the plane during the hour's stay in Panama. Now, as the others busied themselves with preparations for a new day, he remained in his seat.

Banking over Colombia, the pilot locked into the Quito radio beam. With the course set, the plane flew steadily and surely into the new day. Ecuador's capital city lay some 9,500 feet high in the Andes Mountains, and the radio signal was like a celestial carpet down which the jet was moving. The morning was clear, and soon the great mountain peaks were lifting their backs toward the speeding jet. Snow, virgin and white, covered the sleeping volcanoes.

Jon finally moved. He couldn't resist the sight of the humping, beautiful mountains. As his eyes lovingly swept across the Andes, his mind returned once again to his destination. He was going home. A part of him didn't really want to go back to Quito, but he felt as if he had no choice in the matter. He was almost schizophrenic in his attitude toward returning home.

Born in Ecuador, the first child of missionary parents, he loved the country—the long hikes and difficult climbs into the mountains—the smell of frying pork on countless street corners—the fun-filled summers on the coast, and winter after winter studying in school.

He loved his parents; they were strong-minded people, kind and good. But he was puzzled about their work and couldn't fully understand their devotion to God's service. While in high school and still living at home, Jon had seriously pondered his parents' vocation. Somehow their insistence on serving God as missionaries seemed a mystery to him.

His dad had a master's degree in engineering and without too much more effort there could have been additional degrees. An engineer of his caliber could have held any number of important positions, pulled down any salary, but instead he was content to spend his years working at a missionary radio station. Having just completed his requirements for a degree in Latin American studies, Jon was starting to appreciate his parents' desire to work for something other than a monthly paycheck. But he was not satisfied with their reason for coming to Quito, working for radio station HCJB, taking an unimportant place.

When the pilot announced the time for the Quito landing, Jon sensed a conflict deep within his own heart. The excitement of going home was almost physical, and his anticipation of seeing his parents was all joy. But still there was the doubt, the puzzle, the question. He laid his head back on the smudged pillow rest. His long blond hair curled at the ends, and he wondered briefly if his mom would think it too long. But his mind passed over that and came back to essentials.

Didn't Dad understand that service to God meant taking a backseat, losing out on a good salary, not being in on the real exciting advances in engineering? As a teenager Jon hadn't been able to articulate these thoughts, but now he was a man, and he intended to find out exactly what motivated his parents. Service to God? Yes. But that wasn't enough of an answer for him.

Swinging gently over the Ecuadorian countryside, the plane entered its final approach to the Quito airfield. Jon turned to look out the window and caught sight of "his" mountain, Mount Cotopaxi, just off the wing tip.

Cotopaxi! Would he ever forget the glorious day he had stood on her summit? Over 19,500 feet of mountain—mountain he had struggled to conquer. The perfectly shaped beauty stood at the far end of Quito, looking like a giant's vanilla ice-cream cone. The world's highest active volcano, Jon had often longed to climb her glacial sides as she had slumbered over the landscape. Then he had had his chance when the mountain climbing club at his school had set Cotopaxi as its goal.

Led by their enthusiastic teacher, the boys had reached the summit. After five years, Jon still recalled the physical strain of the adventure and the spiritual excitement of the triumph. Within seconds the mountain had vanished from sight and below them lay Quito, stretched along the base of the extinct volcano Pichincha.

Jon had climbed Pichincha many times, often alone. Sometimes he and his brother had taken their guns; occasionally they had even pulled their mom up the rutted pathway leading to the top. Swaying, fragrant eucalyptus trees were still visible on the mountainside, but Jon noted bare spots. Planted on the ridge were man-made steel trees—television towers which Jon did not remember from his youth. Television had come to Quito and man had taken his antennas up the ancient mountain.

Now the jet was flying low over the Pan American Highway leading into the city. Pavement had replaced the cobblestones Jon had known, and he couldn't spot one donkey among all the fast-moving European cars. Sweeping low over the fence, the giant plane touched down on the runway. Jon was home.

Emotion-filled Ecuadorian families were the first to stand when the pilot braked in front of customs. Pushing forward, they strained to be on home soil. They were followed by blasé businessmen who took down their briefcases and turned toward the exit. Next came the tourists, their new camera cases bumping against the seats as they casually moved down the aisle. Most of the in-transit passengers decided to see the Quito airport and they too filed through the exit doors. Jon was the last to leave.

As the passengers left the cabin, heavy suitcases were being flung carelessly from the cargo space onto parked motor carts. Five thousand fertilized chicken eggs received better treatment, but boxes of imported English chocolates were treated worse than the baggage. The luggage load grew higher and higher until the stacks of suitcases almost toppled.

But the crew was rushed and so they took a chance. Onto the top they added the final load: great sacks of mail. Gray bag followed gray bag until twenty-three bulging sacks teetered out of balance on the carts. Mail from all over the world: letters addressed in German, Spanish, English, Russian, Swedish, Japanese, Greek, Chinese; business letters, bills, form letters, magazines, inquiries, family notes—deaths, births, marriages, divorces; propaganda, appeals, statements. Envelopes written in smeared ink, typed on new machines, penciled by children, neatly spelled out or almost illegible. Teenagers telling about school, dads asking about home, mothers seeking news about grandbabies, businessmen working on prices, adventurers inquiring about gold, oil-company men checking on work assignments. Hundreds and hundreds of letters intended for people living in Ecuador.

And the majority of the mail was addressed to Box 691, Quito, Ecuador. Their destination? The same as Jon's: radio station HCJB.

# 2

# Rerouted by Duty

Jon's parents arrived late at the airport. Being late was a bad habit they had acquired through the years. Partly it was an adaptation to the Latin culture, because they had learned that to arrive on time was to be first — first at the party, church service, wedding, funeral, or afternoon tea. So to save their precious minutes for important things, they had cultivated the art of the late arrival. Unfortunately this habit had run over into other areas of their lives. Now they found themselves always five or ten minutes behind their busy schedules. But they had determined to be on time for Jon's plane. And they had made a good start toward their goal.

Allison had been pleased that breakfast had been eaten without the phone ringing once. She happily noted this victory.

"What do you think of that, Marty? A whole meal without one phone call." She reached across the table and touched her husband on the arm as she spoke.

Marty looked into his wife's happy brown eyes.

"Makes a nice start to an important day. You have us up before the sun. I doubt if anybody is out of bed yet to call us."

"You know, Marty," laughed Allison, "we're up so early we can have another cup of coffee. How's that for a rare occurrence?" She jumped up and with a jaunty skip went into the kitchen.

Marty watched her disappear. In two weeks she would be having another birthday. The skin under her chin was starting to sag, and the obvious lines around her eyes indicated that she was well into her forties. But Marty marveled at her continued enthusiasm for life and her bright sense of humor which still bubbled and overflowed at the oddest moments. He loved her, and that in itself was a marvelous thing. But even more amazing was the fact that she loved him. After all, twenty-four years of marriage were a long time.

Occasionally he had been almost impossible to live with. Coming to Ecuador as newlyweds, their marital adjustment plus their adaption to HCJB and the new culture had been interwoven. At times, frustrated by his work and depressed with Latin attitudes and philosophies that he found difficult to understand, Marty had taken his anger home and let it spray over Allison. Those were ugly experiences for both of them, but perhaps necessary ones. Sometimes she would be quiet and only listen. On other occasions she would answer back, giving him argument for argument. Often she would identify with his discontentment and, in so doing, give him valuable support.

In their early years with the mission he had had a mistakenly romantic view of missionary life and an unrealistic concept of marriage. Wiping the false glamour from the mission picture had been painful for Marty, but he was thankful he had come out on the other side. Becoming a pragmatist, he now knew that truth is preeminently to be tested by the practical consequences of belief.

Once the storm of adjustment was over he began to live his life on a very realistic level. And it was the same with his marriage, except there still remained the thrill of love — an amazing thing to Marty. And because he was an honest man, he had to admit to moments when he was overcome by the thrill of missionary engineering. But now it was an authentic excitement, one which had its roots in truth. He liked that and he liked his marriage.

At this point in his thinking the phone rang. Marty rarely answered the telephone because of a slight hearing loss which made it difficult to understand voices over the line. Also, he knew Allison loved to visit on the phone, so he let it ring a couple more times before he reluctantly rose and answered.

Two phones were sitting side by side on the desk. One was the Quito city phone. The other receiver was connected to an internal HCJB system which linked all the missionary homes plus the many business offices, various language divisions, engineering sections, television, hospital, and even the Pifo transmitter site some fifteen miles from Quito. This time the call came from the hospital.

"Do you think that Allison could run down to the hospital for just a moment, Marty?" The pleasant voice on the other end of the line belonged to the nursing director. Trained in Canada, she was doing an efficient job as head of the nursing staff.

"I realize Jon is coming in this morning," she continued, "but Carmen is on second floor and was asking for Allison all last night. The plane won't be in for another couple of hours, and I'm sure Allison will want to see her. Just have her come upstairs."

The steady buzz in his ear told Marty that the conversation was completed. Glancing at his watch, he noticed that the caller was correct, almost to the minute. Exactly two hours until the plane touched down.

He knew Allison would want to talk with Carmen, the girl who had been working for them for three years. Allison had been very disappointed about six weeks ago when the girl had asked permission to quit. She liked Carmen's work and really didn't want to go through all the trouble of finding another maid.

But Carmen had left and Ana had taken her place. The quiet older woman was capable, but both Allison and Marty missed Carmen's happy singing in the kitchen. He wondered for a moment why the girl was in the hospital, and hoped it wasn't anything serious.

"Here darling, here's the hot coffee," Allison announced as she came back to the table.

"Didn't you hear the phone ringing?"

"Did it ring? No, didn't hear a thing. I was talking with Ana about lunch. Guess I was so excited about Jon coming that I wasn't paying attention to little bell noises!"

"The call was for you. Apparently Carmen is in the hospital and wants to talk with you. Don't you think you'd better run down to see her?"

As Marty stood up, his thoughts shifted to the engineering building where he knew a number of urgent papers were waiting on his desk.

"Carmen? In the hospital?" Allison's cup paused midway to her mouth. "What's the matter with her?"

"I don't know. But she wants to talk to you. By the way, Allison, tell them at the accounting office that we'll take care of her bill. We can do that much for her."

He glanced around the neat living room, wondering if he should take along his work folder. He had decided to stop at his desk and do some work while Allison was in the hospital.

That was the way their mornings always went. A nurse, Allison worked five mornings a week at the hospital but was on vacation for Jon's days in Quito.

"What time is it?" Allison jumped up, suddenly anxious about her time schedule. Reassured when she heard they had almost two hours until Jon's plane would land, she said, "Let me give the place a final check and then we can walk down the hill together." And then, because she loved her husband and was excited over the return of her firstborn son, she gave Marty a moist kiss on his cheek and turned with a chuckle as he reached out for her. She ran down the hall, checking the perfectly clean apartment.

Five minutes later they were walking in the direction of the HCJB grounds. It was an early July morning, a beautiful Andean day, and Marty and Allison could see two volcanic peaks outlined by the equatorial sun. A familiar sight, it was one they continually enjoyed.

It was pleasant to walk at this hour. Before the street was paved, they had walked in the dust in the dry season and in the mud in the wet season. But now they followed an elegant sidewalk which ran down the middle of the street. Allison always felt it was an un-

usual place for a sidewalk, but it certainly made walking a lot more fun. Unfortunately, the pavement ended just short of the radio station, so for a minute or two Allison skipped over the potholes. Marty walked around them with more dignity.

They came to the edge of the mission compound. *Compound.* Neither Marty nor Allison liked the word. It sounded colonial, stuffy, set apart. An unfortunate word. But a radio station has to have buildings, and it certainly makes it more convenient to establish the large operation in one location. A city block contained the bulk of the HCJB "compound."

When the couple reached the far end of the lot, they passed a fairly new structure which had been built to house the entire Bible institute correspondence work carried on for Spanish listeners to the radio station. Red and wine-colored geraniums gave a happy welcome, as the two passed on their way to the entrance of the station.

Marty took Allison's hand and gave it a tight squeeze.

"Meet you here in one hour?"

"One hour?" echoed Allison. "I won't be that long."

"Want to bet?" teased Marty. He knew that his wife could spend all morning in the hospital and be convinced that she'd been gone only twenty minutes. Releasing her hand, he made it definite.

"See you in an hour."

Allison turned, walked across the street, and entered the mission hospital.

Shortly after Marty and Allison had come to Ecuador, an Indian hostel clinic had been opened. Allison loved her daily contact with the folks who came to the clinic. If she hadn't been busily raising two sons, she would have been more actively involved in the next step of the medical ministry: rural clinics. By the time the first evangelical hospital in Ecuador had been built, both Jon and his brother were in school and Allison could work each morning in the outpatient clinic.

Through the years she had met scores of fascinating people as they came as patients to the Rimmer Memorial Hospital. She had had a part in treating high-government officials, members of religious orders, working-class folk, the destitute, a large group of missionaries, and a number of families from the foreign community.

Now as Allison hurried through the downstairs hall, she passed the emergency section, the pharmacy, laboratory, and X-ray room. She could hear the clatter of breakfast dishes, and the moist warm air from the laundry told her that the washing machines had been working for hours.

Quickly climbing the stairs, she stopped at the nurses' station to inquire about Carmen. Everyone was busy and only a vague wave of a hand indicated in which direction Carmen could be found. Allison was surprised at the section pointed out, but she turned left and seconds later entered Carmen's room.

Carmen had been waiting for her. Smiling wanly, she immediately began to explain things to Allison. A good listener, Allison had a sympathetic heart. She stood quietly and let the girl talk.

"This is my story. I want you to know it, Senora. I know you want to hear it. Please try to understand what I'm saying. I didn't want to deceive you, but I

was so ashamed and I didn't know how to tell you. But
now it's over and I can speak about it, so please stay
and listen. Is there a chair? Good. Sit down and hear
me. This is my story:

"It was cold last November. Remember? We had a
fire every day because the rain and the winds made
things so uncomfortable. I loved to make the fire. The
heat closed out the cold. But I always hated to go home
at the end of a rainy day. My coat never seemed warm
enough after the sun had gone down. I had your soup
ready. I didn't want to leave, but it was time.

"Then you gave me the coat. I was thankful, for it
would mean protection from the rain. That was the
night then, the night you gave me the coat, that was the
night my story started and happened and ended. So,
you can see, it is a short story. It all took place on a
cold, wet, November night. When I left your house, I
was just one of many Ecuadorian maids going home.
When I came back the next morning, I was something
else.

"The coat was red, bright red. It made me happier to
leave the house because I felt as if the red color somehow made me warmer than the thin blue coat I had
been wearing. I felt proud to have something new, and
it did fit well, didn't it? I mean, it looked nice on me.

"Of course, there is always my back. But when I
stood and looked straight into your mirror I couldn't
see my back, and I pretended that I was perfect and tall
and pretty. A lovely young senorita in a new red coat.
That's why all this came about — because I forgot who I
was and what I was, and I really believed that I was
attractive and beautiful. Just for one night I felt whole.

The red coat did that for me on that cold November evening.

"From your house to the bus stop isn't very far. In the dark I kept stumbling, but I made sure my coat didn't get muddy. I didn't have long at the bus stop. That was good, or at least I thought so at the time, because it meant I wouldn't get too wet. The news-paper I was using to keep my hair dry was starting to drip and sag, so I dropped it in the dark when the bus came.

"There weren't many people on the bus that night. I was glad because that meant I could sit down. I'd much rather sit. My back doesn't hurt when I'm sitting; it isn't as noticeable either. I sat near the back but not all the way back. I made sure the seat was dry and clean since I didn't want to spot the new coat.

"So I sat down and soon the fare collector came down the aisle and asked for my centavos, and he said, 'Hey! Look at the chicken. A red chicken. Say, seno-rita, you must be someone special to be out in the rain with a new red coat.'

"And because there were so few people on the bus and no others to collect money from, he came and sat down next to me. I was so happy. I didn't even play at being shy. I looked right at him and said, 'Red chickens like wet, cold nights.'

"Wasn't I shameful? I know I was, and yet, can you understand what his attention meant to me?

"You know how our men can talk. They do not fumble for words, nor do they discuss silly things like American men. No, our men know how to talk to girls. 'That red coat makes your eyes sparkle and your teeth how they shine and your hair—ah, your hair. There are no words to tell how black and bright your hair is tonight.'

"And then he took my hand and held it and said: 'I'll be right back. See, more crazy people out on this cold night. More coins for the company. But save this seat, little one. I'll come back to my chicken.'

"My chicken. That's what he had called me. In all of my twenty-two years that was the first time any man or boy had used that endearment with me. The boys on the street would call me names, but only names which went well with my back. My brothers' friends were kinder. They were polite but never did they flirt with me like they did with my sister. For the first time somebody looked into my eyes and held my hands. I was excited. This was fun, harmless fun on a city bus in November.

"He kept his promise. He came back.

"I'm sorry. Isn't this the day Jon comes? But you do have more time, don't you? Please stay, Senora Allison. You and only you have come to see me. I have brought such shame to my family. Stay and I will quickly tell the rest.

"Can you not guess what went on that night? Riding the bus to the end of the line and then back again. Sitting and laughing and having a wonderful time. His uncle owned the bus and was driving it. This old man would look in the mirror and his tired eyes would burn with past memories. He knew what was coming. I think I must have known also, but I could not stop. Such is life.

"It was midnight when we parked for coffee. The old man pulled the bus up on the sidewalk by the café. His nephew took me by the arm and led me to the steps. I had been thinking of nothing but the fun of his talk. As he helped me down the steps, his uncle twisted in his seat.

" 'Ah, so my nephew likes a broken chicken. Does he think a damaged chicken tastes sweeter?'

"I kept my eyes down and didn't look up. Everything had been so good and now it was over. But he did not let me down.

" 'Uncle, uncle, this is my little red hen. A bent wing does not keep a chicken from laying eggs.'

"His laugh washed away my sadness and fear. As he lifted me off the bus steps I felt my heart flying higher than it has ever flown. This was to be my night. And it was, senora, my night.

"But how could it be? One night and no more. How foolish. That was all, though. Just the one night in the gay little café at the bus stop. Where did he go? To the coast? Perhaps to Colombia? I do not know. Such is life. Now there is nothing but my red coat and —

"That must end my story. Here comes the nurse. She is bringing her. How tiny and brown and perfect she is. Take her, senora. Hold her. Her back is not bent; she is not marked. She is mine, a daughter.

"Senora, please do not look so sad. Everything will be fine. I will come back to you and work for you, and my baby will come also. God will help my family to forget this shame, and I pray to Him that they will love this child — this girl-child born to the little red chicken with the broken wing."

Allison knew she was going to cry the minute she held the baby in her arms. And she did cry. She wept for the baby, another illegitimate baby in a country having many fatherless children.

She wept for Carmen. She did not doubt that Carmen was a Christian girl. She had heard her testimony and had seen her baptized; she was a member of an evangelical church. But Allison knew what this would mean to the girl who would be put under discipline by the church. She prayed that the Christians would be loving and kind, but she wasn't sure.

When she stopped crying and handed the perfectly formed child to her mother, it suddenly dawned on Allison that she had been fooled. Completely. This badly crippled girl had hidden her secret well beneath the full, pleated skirts which Allison had given her.

Only when the baby began to nurse noisily did Allison remember what day it was. With a promise to return, she turned and left Carmen. A glance at the clock above the nurses' station reassured her. She had been there an hour and five minutes — still plenty of time to meet the plane. She didn't know that Marty had also become involved and would be even later than she.

After watching Allison cross the street, Marty had stopped long enough to greet the gateman and then had walked toward the engineering building. To his right, frond-laden palm trees were stately, receiving the early morning sun while dew danced on the grass growing around their bases. Glancing down the green row, Marty noted that the door to a small building was still closed. Too early for prayer meeting.

He always made an effort to attend the prayer times, but he was no longer bound to formal prayer hours. Without any conscious effort, his mind would slip into conversations with God. He had been communicating with Him in this way for years. He liked sharing his thoughts in this casual manner and rather suspected that God liked it too. Before he reached the steps leading to his office, Marty was already deep in conversation.

*Well, Lord, it looks like a nice day, weatherwise and in ways important to Allison and myself.*

*Thank You for letting Jon come home. We've missed him. I'm anxious to talk with him, catch his thinking about You. Help us to make these ten days count.*

*Help me to listen to Jon. Really listen.*

*I always tended to do most of the talking when Jon was around. I think I'll be more relaxed around the boy now. Thank You, Lord, for helping me to tone down.*

*Jon is a good boy. I love him.*

Marty was halfway up the stairs when he saw an Ecuadorian control operator coming out of the studio building. He turned and retraced his steps so that he could greet the boy and ask about his family. Even as he shook the young man's hand, Marty's stream of prayer continued along, uninterrupted.

*Lucas is a good boy too, Lord. But it's harder for him.*

*Give him the strength he needs to choose to walk Your way. I like him and so do You.*

*Might be a good idea to have him up for supper while Jon's here. Remind me to ask Allison.*

*Bless this boy, Lord. Work in the lives of each control operator we have. Meet their needs. Thank You.*

Marty gave Lucas a warm hug and then took the stairs two at a time. He wanted to check over a report he'd typed out the night before. And if he were quick enough, he might catch Ricardo and have a talk with him. He'd been intending to talk with Ricardo for the past week. This extra hour would be a perfect opportunity.

*Lord, I need Your wisdom in working something out with Ricardo.*

*I don't want him to leave. He's great and a really good second hand to me.*

*Am I selfish in wanting him to stay here? Perhaps. But he's good. Reliable. I can't count on the next man being as cooperative as Ricardo.*

*I know he needs more money. That's the problem. He can earn more if he works for the oil company in the jungle. And down there he'd have a Bible class going before his bags were unpacked and his bed made. I know that, Lord.*

*But I need him. Let me know what I should do. He won't leave without my consent. That's the trouble. He wants to go, I know that.*

*OK. Give me the grace to let him go.*

Marty fitted his key into the door and walked into the large working area used by the engineering staff. Crossing to the back of the room, he opened the door to his office. He was a neat man and he glanced with pleasure around his small domain. On his brown desk, a row of technical journals and books was tightly stacked between two hand-carved Ecuadorian llamas, a gift from Ricardo. The sheet he had typed the night before was still in the typewriter, and as Marty sat down he pulled the paper from the carriage. He read it quickly to check for any mistakes. There weren't any.

### HCJB Technical Report

On Christmas day, 1931, our one radio studio could be found in the half-finished sheep shed in Quito, Ecuador. We went on the air with a 250-watt transmitter and broadcast two hours a day in one language. Rated at 250 watts of power, the homemade transmitter made missionary news as God's Word was proclaimed from the converted sheep shed, and HCJB became the first missionary radio station in the world.

Now in our fortieth year, there are, in Pifo, one 50,000-watt long-wave, two 50,000-watt shortwave, two 30,000-watt shortwave and three 100,000-watt shortwave transmitters. All except the 100,000-watt transmitters are of HCJB design and were built in Ecuador. Programs and telephone communications are relayed by means of a multichannel microwave system from Quito. Twenty-five steel towers, nearly all of them fabricated in Pifo, support the sixteen curtain antennas. Two diesel engines drive the emergency power generators.

Power for the transmitter installation comes from HCJB's own hydroelectric generating plant another twenty-five miles to the east. There at the town of Papallacta, the river of the same name is harnessed on its way to the Amazon to generate a maximum of 2,000 kilowatts for use in Pifo.

No sheep shed could possibly contain all the equipment now used. The studio building in Quito holds five studios and six control rooms. The largest studio, the "World Radio Chapel," is big enough to hold large choirs, and at one time served as the television studio. The radio studio equipment includes twenty-three broadcast-quality tape recorders, fifteen cartridge tape recorders, and ten broadcast-quality turntables. Five sets of control consoles are of commercial manufacture, while one semiautomated control is of HCJB design and construction.

Satisfied that the report was OK, Marty placed it next to the other material to be left at the secretarial pool. HCJB's administrative offices were right above his head. The president had the end room, and the field director and several assistants occupied the office space running down the hall. Across the hall from them were the secretaries' rooms, and Marty would slip his report into their receiving basket before he had to meet Allison.

Now, where would he find Ricardo? Probably over at the television building. The largest and newest structure on the HCJB compound was located right behind and somewhat above the building where Marty now sat. This week Ricardo was doing some repair work on the control panel. He usually came in early and checked over the equipment. A phone call confirmed Marty's deduction, and moments later Ricardo walked into the engineering room. Marty stood up immediately and gave the man a warm handshake.

These two men were friends. Marty knew this and so did the Ecuadorian. They made an interesting contrast as they stood in front of Marty's desk.

The North American was tall and lean, his eyes were blue and clear. Furrowed lines ran back and forth across his forehead, speaking of thoughtful maturity. His sandy blond hair was still youthfully abundant, but the sideburns he was growing had come in all dusted with gray. Deeply etched around his mouth testified to the fact that Marty frequently smiled—a warm, generous smile. He shared it with everyone. He looked middle-aged, but not in a used, wornout way. Handsomeness had come with his maturing. Even the addition of glasses had added to his confidence-inspiring appearance.

But to his Spanish-speaking friends he seemed huge and his size eleven shoes were mammoth boats. From his six-foot-three-inch height, he looked down on Ricardo. In fact, he looked down on most Ecuadorian people, although a doctor friend was taller than he. But that man was an exception.

When he and Allison first came to Ecuador, he had felt awkward, out of place, because of his size. But everyone had been so cordial and friendly that he soon forgot that he towered over everyone in almost every room. This morning he wasn't even conscious of being taller that Ricardo. But he was—inches taller.

Ricardo was about the same age as Marty but his face had escaped the aging process. With brown eyes the same color as his dark hair and neatly trimmed moustache, his round face betrayed Indian ancestry now generations removed. A clear smile equaled Marty's for sincerity. A Christian for many years, Ricardo was as devoted to sharing Christ with others as any foreign missionary working in his country.

Ricardo had been born near the town of Pelileo. Years after he left the area, his hometown was devastated by an earthquake. At that time the HCJB mobile transmitter and medical staff were rushed to the scene of the disaster. Before the quake, the town had a population of three thousand. Afterward not a house was left standing. The church was a tumbled pile of stone blocks. Its huge iron bell lay on top of the ruin—mouth to the sky—clapper silent. Thousands of bodies lay crushed beneath tons of rubble; only three hundred people escaped alive.

Radio station HCJB became the communication center for a nation. The president of the country went to the site, and his message was rebroadcast on the short-wave and long-wave bands.

When Ricardo was growing up, the countryside was

a peaceful farm community. As a young boy he had cared for his father's few cows and followed the wooden plow, breaking up the brown chunks of dirt. But the farm had been a poor one, so when Ricardo was ten years old his family moved down into the jungle. They found an empty house just beyond the town of Shell Mera, and it was there that Ricardo grew to manhood.

Their wooden home faced the town square, and during the warm evenings he had played soccer there with his friends. His father's income had not increased with the move, so Ricardo tried to help his family by polishing shoes. Many little boys needed extra money, so business wasn't too good for Ricardo. But he grew up free and happy. His parents had enough to buy food and pay the rent, so, except for when they had to purchase extra medicines or school supplies, they managed well on their limited income. Only a few times in his boyhood did Ricardo really feel the lack of money. One of those times had a direct connection with HCJB.

One afternoon a very strange visitor entered the village square. A large sound bus had been driven down from Quito and parked right in the middle of Ricardo's soccer field. Curious about this odd-shaped vehicle, the boy joined his friends in pressing around it for a closer look.

It had been a hard drive from the capital city because the HCJB sound bus had had to cross rivers and bump over almost impassable roads. Rarely did anyone make the drive without some good reason, and it wasn't long before Ricardo learned the purpose of the visit.

The men had come to tell the people about God, and soon began to sing and talk. Ricardo was fascinated. At that moment a desire to know God was born in his young heart.

When the man standing beside the truck said he would sell Spanish Bible portions to anyone wanting them, Ricardo immediately began hunting through his torn pockets for a coin left over from his shoe-shining. There was none. Turning, he pushed through the crowd and in less than a minute was at home. But his mother could not help him; she too had nothing.

Ricardo walked down the steps of his house and stood on the edge of the crowd. Next to him was an older man, a village friend. This man was a Christian who knew Ricardo, and he guessed rightly that the boy had no money.

"Buenos dias, Ricardo. Have you been listening to the words of God?"

"Buenos dias, senor. Yes, I have. And I want to buy a part of the Bible."

"Well, go right ahead," urged the understanding man. He put a few centavos into Ricardo's hand.

The boy shot a quick "gracias" over his shoulder and pushed through the crowd until he reached the North American who was standing at the back of the bus. The exchange took place.

Within days the boy had read and reread the selections from the gospels of Mark and John. Without any struggle he found himself understanding the life of Jesus and realizing that he too could follow the Man of Galilee. What he had purchased in the plaza one late afternoon became his treasure, and the God he had found became his Companion.

As he grew older he decided that he wanted the

entire Bible. He had heard that it was possible to buy one in the large mountain town of Ambato.

"I am told that there is a man in this neighborhood who speaks of God and sells His Word. Can you show me his house?"

Ricardo stood on the corner of a narrow cobblestone street. In both directions the closed houses pushed up to the very edge of the street. While riding into Ambato on the top of a large fat bus, he had reached out and touched the buildings. He had jumped down when the bus stopped at the intersection. From the vague directions given him at home, he assumed that this was the district in which the man lived.

"Bibles? Yes. That house down there. The fourth one. You can buy your Bible there."

As a teenager Ricardo had found enough odd jobs to augment the family purse. He had regularly saved out a small portion of the coins until there were enough to make the trip up into the mountains. Now he made his purchase and spent a couple of hours visiting with the Christian man who had sold him the Bible. Just as Ricardo was leaving, the man remembered something important.

"Listen. Near your village live a man and his wife. He is a pilot and his wife a nurse, and they are going to build a hangar and home there. Soon the man will be flying supplies and missionaries to their mission's jungle stations. Why don't you stop and visit this couple? They will welcome you and I know you will like them. I'm sure they will help you learn more and more of God's Word."

Ricardo was anxious to meet anybody who could

share in his desire to understand God, so on his way back home he stopped at the Missionary Aviation Fellowship property. Not only did the foreigners welcome Ricardo and set up a weekly Bible study with him, but they also gave him work and trained him. He helped build their home and the hangar for the plane. Then he learned how to do electrical work and was entrusted with mechanical problems.

In the early 1950s Ricardo left Shell Mera and went to work for radio station HCJB. His first assignment was to help with the construction of the transmitter sites outside the small mountain town of Pifo. There Marty first met this man who had remained his friend for so many years.

Twenty years of HCJB's history had occurred before Marty and Ricardo met. Both men were familiar with the interesting story of the "birth" of the station.

It was an impossible place to put a transmitter! Or so the missionaries thought on first glimpse of the building. Just a mud-walled, half-finished sheep shed, boasting a corrugated-tin roof, with only a dirt floor underneath, it had been stuck out among the stables years before. It was more used to the sound of the bleating of lambs than to the modern cacophony of radio broadcasting. But there came the day when, duly fixed up with whitewash and a cement floor, the shed actually saw the technical birth of missionary broadcasting.

That was back on Christmas Day, 1931. It was enough of a national event that the president of Ecuador inaugurated the station. Rated at 250 watts power, the homemade transmitter made Ecuadorian radio history. It was the first broadcast station on the equator with regular daily programs.

A hole punched through the thick adobe walls of a hallway closet in the missionary residence provided an observation window for the control operator. And the living room became a working study by the simple process of installing a microphone there. Assigned frequencies in the long-wave and major shortwave bands, the pioneer missionary station's own technical men built several sister stations to the original 250-watter.

As the 1930s progressed, the station began to be heard beyond the limits of Quito — out in the provinces, then beyond Ecuador into nearby republics, and finally throughout the entire South American continent. Before 1940, the programs were being heard in the United States.

The Ecuadorian government ruled in 1940 that HCJB would have to move outside Quito's city limits. After nine years in the converted sheep shed a new location had to be sought. Because the station wished to increase its power to 100,000 watts, that meant a major move. A cabbage patch was purchased on the northern limits of Quito, and Easter Sunday saw another president of Ecuador honoring HCJB by attending the dedication services.

Since the increase in power meant that the signal could cover a large percentage of the globe, new languages began to be added to the broadcast schedule. During the decade of the '40's over 40,000 hours of gospel broadcasting were sent out on the 10,000-watt transmitter.

Seasonal atmospheric changes, local interferences, the weaknesses of receiving sets, and the knowledge that God could use radio waves to reach the world's 300 million shortwave listeners, were the motivating

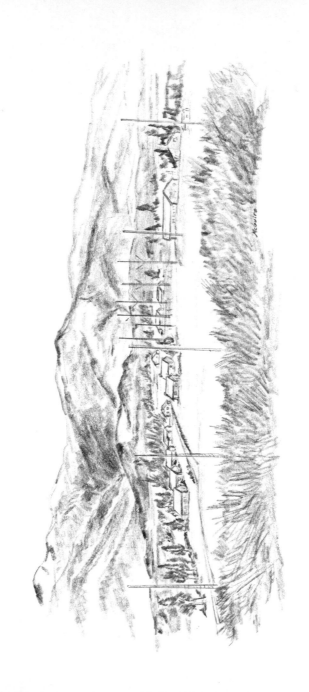

forces that impelled the HCJB staff to increase their radio power to 100,000 watts. Difficulties of design and construction were technical problems, so the engineers were given the responsibility of building the two 50,000-watt transmitters.

Fifteen miles from Quito, forty-five acres of pastureland were purchased and transformed into the transmitter site. Two hundred and twenty-two boxes and crates of radio equipment necessary for the initial stages of building the giant transmitters were already in Ecuador when Ricardo moved onto the grounds in Pifo. His first work assignment was to help with the construction of new homes for the technical staff and also with new buildings for the transmitters and diesel plant.

By the end of 1952 the diesel power plant had been installed, the cornerstone of the new building had been laid, and bases for the new antenna towers had been built, with the first tower sections erected. During the years of construction work at Pifo, Ricardo and Marty spent many working hours together and came to know each other well.

While living in Pifo, Ricardo had married. His wife was a town girl whom he had met at a weekly Bible study. Although Ruth was four years older, he was attracted by her gay spirit and love of Christ. She made him a good wife, and for eighteen years had shared in his work. But they now had six children, and Marty knew this was the reason Ricardo would have to change jobs.

The two men spent thirty minutes discussing various work assignments and potential engineering problems. Then Marty turned the conversation to the subject he had not wanted to approach.

"Ricardo, I think you should take that job offer—the one from the oil company. I've been praying about it, trying to sort out all the advantages and disadvantages. What you told me is true. You and Ruth need extra income now that the children are older. I understand that. And this new offer is a good one, a well-paying opportunity for you. Go ahead, Ricardo, take it."

Ricardo was grateful to Marty for understanding the situation. He had decided weeks ago to resign from HCJB, but he did not want to leave until he was sure that Marty was in agreement with his withdrawal. He was sorry to leave Quito but looked forward to the new assignment. Both he and Ruth felt confident of God's direction in their lives and were thankful for the prospect of being able to meet their expenses.

The two men discussed the completion of certain projects and decided that Ricardo could probably leave within the month. They also talked of a possible replacement, and the sincere offer was made of a place for him if the oil-company job proved a disappointment. There were many details to think about and Marty became so absorbed, that he forgot his promise to Allison. When she finally stood in the doorway, Ricardo had just left. And Allison knew that if the plane was on schedule, they would be late.

"Who was it that was going to take longer than she thought?" teased Allison. Usually the last one out of the door, she couldn't be angry with Marty. As they walked to their Volkswagen, they both saw and heard the giant jet as it skimmed over the FM transmitter which towered over the Quito compound. It was less than a five-minute drive to the airport. They might get there before the plane stopped for unloading.

But they didn't and when Jon finally left the plane he couldn't find his parents in the waiting crowd. Somehow their not being there tickled him. He could picture his dad making a mad dash through traffic and he was sure they would be standing outside the door to the customs room.

They were, and the joy of being home again washed away all his misgivings. His mother was laughing as Jon swept her off the ground, and his dad's whole being told Jon that coming home was the right thing to have done. Only ten days, but they wouldn't be wasted.

Setting his mom down, and still holding her hand, he embraced his father. The warmth of his dad's grasp on his shoulder conveyed to Jon the older man's love and confidence. Jon was glad to be home again.

# 3

# Response Overflows

The presidential palace in Quito is a building full of wonders. Author John Gunther describes the structure as the most attractive palace of its kind on the whole continent of South America. In one room, large enough for sixty-four guests at a single table, a frieze of portraits of all the presidents of Ecuador stretches under a heavy gold-ornamented ceiling.

The entrance hall is solidly inlaid with large mosaic panels created by the country's best-known artist, Guayasamin. Within are beautifully appointed rooms, while the outside of the building always looks as if it has just been given a new coat of white paint. The palace majestically faces the central square, Plaza Independencia.

A tourist, enthralled by the drama and movement around the presidential palace would probably miss a less-imposing structure which stands with its back pressed against the palace. This is unfortuante, for during the daylight hours and well into the night the post office is a fascinating place. The letters which are constantly flying from hand to table to box are paper missives filled with drama.

The truck which receives the mail from the airport is as brightly painted as the plane from which the sacks have so recently been thrown. In a matter of minutes the bags have made their transfer, and the driver turns his truck out onto the Pan American Highway.

Driving rapidly and without caution, he skims around a circular monument which stands at the end of the airfield fence. Two mammoth oxen, molded from concrete, plow the soil upon which the city has placed them, eternally committed to the earth. In their set stance they speak of dignity and silence, the dignity and silence of the Andean Indian.

Constantly using his horn, and passing cars, the Ecuadorian driver has raced this way too often to be impressed by the scenes outside his window. But he should take notice, for the city of Quito is exploding: growth is everywhere. Grimy, stained, one-story mud dwellings are being torn down. In their place are paved streets, new apartment houses, large stores, and fine office buildings. Others, passing this way, note the distinctive Spanish flavor of this rapidly changing city. Hopefully the new construction will not erase the colonial image which has allowed Quito to remain so obviously a part of her past.

His thoughts elsewhere, the driver almost misses seeing the policeman who is directing traffic with movements of his body. Just in time, the mail truck slams to a halt. Turning sideways, the human traffic light permits the vehicle to continue.

As the truck enters the downtown section of Quito, the volume of traffic forces the chauffeur to drive more sanely. The streets have narrowed. Two cars, side by side, fill the narrow passageway. Pedestrians are every-where. Fashionably dressed matrons push along ahead of slower-moving poncho-draped Indians.

Along the route to the post office are crowded the city buildings, uniformly the same color in their white-washed coverings. Many of the structures are hundreds of years old, built by the Spaniards when they wrestled the city from the Incas.

Twenty minutes after leaving the north end of Quito, the mail arrives at the post office entrance. No parking space is available so the driver successfully blocks traffic while barefooted men unload the gray sacks. While the mailbags are disappearing into the building, the jangle of car horns becomes increasingly louder as other drivers urge the truck to move. Suddenly silence drops over the scene. The truck has unblocked the street; the letters are inside the post office.

The mail sacks end their journey just outside the sorting-room door, where they rest in crazily leaning piles until the proper man comes to drag them into a large, dimly-lighted room. Heaving them up in the air and then shaking them quickly, the post office em-ployee dumps their contents onto a large unpainted central table. A wooden fence around the table's edge causes the sprayed contents to slide to an abrupt stop before they can be lost on the floor.

As each bag is emptied, a cloud of dust and paper scraps fills the air. This storm dictates the dress of the eight Ecuadorian women who sit with their backs to the main table as they sort the mail and put every piece in its proper cubbyhole. Brightly printed head scarfs are wound around their heads, mouths and noses, providing ample protection against the flying bits of paper.

A young boy, working at the central table, scoops up

the mail and then scatters it by the armloads before the waiting women. Deftly and quickly they shoot the letters into the hundreds of slots climbing the walls before their eyes.

Box 691 is more than one small waiting space. Mail for HCJB is of such quantity that it requires two large openings plus a huge basket container.

The eight women, all well through their middle years, have handled mail for decades and have seen the letters addressed to Box 691 grow in volume. As HCJB expanded, so did their mundane task; yet, they do not complain at the increase in mail. They have come to appreciate the Spanish broadcasts over the evangelical station and in recent years have invited HCJB-TV into their homes. Because they value the programs of HCJB, they have come to look upon the handling of Box 691 mail as a special service, their way of saying "thank you."

The other side of the cubbyholed wall is covered by little brown doors with rusted hinges. The doors are constantly being lifted, the mail taken out, and the doors slammed shut again. From this wall the mail is taken up a short flight of steps and left with the postmistress. Since she finds it an impossible task to stuff all the letters for HCJB into the final box, she has devised a special system of placing every piece of mail that she can into Box 691, and then carefully piling the remainder onto a leaning table.

Two or three times a day an HCJB employee turns the key in the post office box, takes out the letters, and puts them into his black carrying case. As he walks through the crowded lobby and out into the busy street, the box is being filled once again.

# 4

# Reminiscences

Jon woke suddenly, without recalling where he was. It was dark in the room and unfamiliar shapes stood like sentinels in the corners. A dog began to bark somewhere in the night as Jon turned on his side. He was cold, so he began searching for the control to the electric blanket. Then he abruptly remembered that he was in Quito. Turning the switch to medium-high, he lay back, waiting for the warmth to spread over his body. As the heat penetrated through the thin quilt, he found himself relaxing.

He had been tired the night before. Yet, his desire to be with his parents had been stronger than the physical weariness. At first he had felt strange, as if there were barriers between himself and his folks. But his father's relaxed attitude and his mother's excited talk quickly erased any uneasiness. They had spent the day getting reacquainted and making plans for his visit.

For a long time they had discussed the possibility of

taking the train down to Guayaquil, the chief port city of Ecuador. Reminiscing about the only trip they had taken by rail to the coastal area, they debated whether they should repeat it. Jon, who had been fourteen years old at the time, could vividly remember the adventure. It had been like a giant roller-coaster ride from the moment the single streetcarlike train had left the high Andes until it rattled to a stop beside the wide Guayas River.

Amazingly, the train had left the station at the hour stated in the schedule, 6 A.M. Rounding the first corner, it had let forth a great blast, a noise which was to continue for the entire journey. It was necessary. The tracks were continually being emptied and refilled with cows, donkeys, Indians, pigs, children, and chickens. The piercing horn alerted the countryside to the fact that the train was approaching an intersection. Since there were no railroad signals, the horn was essential equipment if the train (known as a *ferrocarril*) were to pass safely over the intersecting highways.

The train tracks ran down Ecuador's beautiful avenue of volcanoes. When Marty and Allison had taken Jon and his brother on the ten-hour trip they had been fortunate in having perfect weather. They clearly saw Mount Chimborazo spreading out along the horizon, its massively crowned summit glistening white in the early morning. It would have been wonderful to have stopped at the foot of the 20,702-foot volcano, but no such treat was allowed. In fact, the engineer was sleeping soundly as the train pulled its own self and forty-five passengers steadily around the base of the giant mountain and continued into the harsh Andean landscape.

For Jon and his brother the best part of the trip came when the sturdy little car reached the Devil's Nose. At this point the tracks plunged thousands of feet down the face of the ageless mountain. Within minutes the *ferrocarril* had left the bleak, windswept peaks behind and entered the green Ecuadorian rain forest. In constructing the route, the men had laid the tracks in U-shaped twists. The descent was so sharp and perilous that it was essential for all trains to back down the slope.

Allison had remained in her seat while everyone else crowded to the windows to watch the view slide beneath them while they ground backward down the steep decline. As the rounded right side of the train hung out over space, Allison felt she was keeping things in balance by remaining on the opposite side where the car brushed against the granite mountain. After this part of the trip, everything else was anticlimactic.

When the journey ended, Jon felt a great weariness from the constant swaying of the train as well as a deep longing for the cool mountains. Guayaquil, a humid, tropical metropolis, was hot and uncomfortable. But it was a beautifully laid-out city and an interesting spot to visit.

However, they decided not to make the trip during Jon's stay, although Marty did have some technical work to do there for the All Ecuador Gospel Network. This department of HCJB is located in Ecuador's largest city and its ministry is to provide gospel program tapes for about one hundred commercial radio stations throughout the country. Their final decision was to drive to Shell. So, with that trip on the schedule, they had all gone to bed.

Jon went back to sleep and didn't wake up again until breakfast was on the table. The fresh naranjilla juice was a treat for him because he hadn't tasted the fruit since leaving Ecuador. The moistly scrambled eggs, fresh bacon, and warm German bread completed the meal.

Shortly the Volkswagen was speeding toward Shell.

"The last time we were in Shell was when Olga died." Allison made the comment in a quiet voice.

"When was that?" questioned Jon. He didn't know who Olga was, but by his mother's reaction he sensed it had been a sad experience.

"About three years ago, wasn't it, Allison?" Marty was driving while Jon sat in the small seat next to the window. Allison, sitting in the back, leaned forward with her arms resting behind her two men.

"Yes, you're exactly right. Three years ago." Allison was a good conversationalist and an even better story-teller. Jon had loved it when he and his brother had talked her into telling a bedtime tale. He knew she was about to tell another story, only this one would be true.

"It was going to be another hot, muggy day. But many days in the Ecuadorian jungle town of Shell are hot and muggy. Olga didn't mind the heat. She began to prepare breakfast and sang to herself as she put out the chipped blue plates. How she loved to cook and work in this tiny apartment. Olga was nineteen years old, a new bride and very happy.

"She had not always been happy. Many years before, her mother had died. It was then her father became bitter. What love he had within, died with his wife. He turned over all the chores to Olga, expecting the child to perform her duties as well as her mature mother had. Hard year followed hard year as Olga worked for her uncompromising father.

"Olga searched for contentment and thought she had found happiness in a young boy just her age. They married and moved into a second-floor apartment.

"On the morning I'm thinking about, she suddenly stopped her singing and turned laughing to face her young husband. How sweet and considerate he was. Not like her father. He stood, in the early morning heat, eager to help her with their meager breakfast.

"And she needed help. Their secondhand gasoline stove was tricky. It often frightened her, for it would spit and refuse to catch fire. She thought of Mary, her friend who had been burned by a stove just like the one she was using. Mary had let the gasoline leak out, and the fumes had exploded in her face. Yes, Olga was afraid to light the one-burner stove. How wonderful to have a husband who was willing to help, a husband who was willing to strike the match and warm the coffee water.

"The family who lived below the newlyweds were eating their breakfast when they heard a loud, explosive-type noise. It was an unusual noise, so they decided to go upstairs and investigate. But, just before reaching the door, they changed their minds. It was probably just a lovers' spat. They returned to their apartment; they didn't want to interfere.

"And so nobody 'interfered' until it was too late. Nobody came until the exploding gasoline stove had performed its lethal act of killing the husband and fatally injuring his young bride.

"When they brought Olga and her dead husband to the Epp Memorial Hospital, both your father and I were there. Everyone knew it was too late to save the life of the badly burned girl. And yet, Olga was destined to live for two more pain-filled weeks — destined to believe that only in Christ is there salvation."

"You know, Jon," Marty picked up the thread of the story, "it was your mother who sat for those two weeks with Olga. We'd gone down to Shell because I had some technical work to do and Allison needed a rest. A burn case is a difficult nursing assignment, but your mother gladly took on the responsibility. I think she must have read continuously to the girl."

Marty swung the car around a large banana truck and then took his place once again in the right lane. It had begun to rain.

"I had to read to her," Allison said. "She was in great pain and the sorrow of her husband's death kept her from sleeping. I read her all the psalms that talk about comfort, God's comfort. I read to her about Jesus, and over and over I talked of His love, the love of God."

When Allison had finished, Jon stared past the rhythmic movements of the windshield wipers and out into the misty Andean morning.

"Why, Mother, did you do it? Weren't those two weeks in Shell supposed to have been your vacation?"

Marty glanced over at his son. Allison was caught off guard. She had never wondered why she had spent that time with Olga. But she knew the answer.

"Because I loved her, Jon, and because she needed me."

"Loved her? How could you have? Why, you didn't even know her." Jon was probing, seeking something from his folks, some basic response.

"No, I didn't know her, at least not the first day. But we soon became friends and I, well, I just loved her, Jon. She was really quite a brave young girl. And she needed me."

"Just before we drive into Shell we'll pass the grave-yard, Jon," Marty answered quietly. "Olga is buried there. It's interesting that she isn't buried inside the gates. No, her grave is outside the actual cemetery. The townspeople believed that she had died outside the gates of heaven. That's because she made a commitment to Jesus Christ and then told everyone about it. I mean everyone—her family, friends, and anyone else who happened to be near her bed. Of course they didn't understand and thought she'd changed her religion. But that didn't have anything to do with what had happened to her. She had just come to trust the one who cared for her and loved her more than anyone else had ever done."

The fog and rain closed in and Marty turned on the yellow headlights. Nobody spoke. Allison rested her head against the back seat and soon went to sleep.

East of the Andes Mountains, four jungle provinces form the region known as the "Oriente." This is Ecuador's frontier and her share of the rim of the vast Amazon River basin. Part of this center of Spanish population has a history as old as Quebec, Boston, and New York City. But only in the past thirty years, as the search for petroleum has opened up the area, has any notable progress been made.

Since 1954, a medical team has been doing what it can to provide compassion and concern for the bodies and the souls of the people in the 30,000-square-mile territory that extends north, south, and east. In 1958 the Epp Memorial Hospital was dedicated and opened in Shell to make the medical and spiritual ministry more effective. The road that leads down from the mountains into the rain forest was constructed by the Shell Oil Company. It is a dirt road, sometimes closed by mud slides, but maintained in fairly good condition by the government.

The Volkswagen carefully drove down the narrow pathway as a life-and-death drama was coming toward the hospital. The car and its passengers would arrive in Shell at the same time as an Indian mother and her child.

\* \* \*

"Oh baby, my baby, please awake! You are so hot and limp. Please wake and cry like you did after your birth. I do not want you to be like this. I want you to be lively instead of deathlike. Please, my baby, please wake!"

But the tiny Indian baby did not respond to the quiet singing of his worried mother. And so the Indian woman slid the baby securely into the worn blanket. Tying the child on her back, she began a journey which she had long considered taking. She started walking to the mission hospital.

Five times before, she had thought of making the long trip. But she had been afraid to go, afraid of the white strangers. Five times before, she had sung her soul-catching lullaby. Five times before, her dear, naked brown babies had died.

But not this time. She would not let this baby die. Even though she was afraid, she would walk the long distance to the hospital. Maybe the strangers could help. Yes, they would help. This baby would not die.

When Marty maneuvered the car around the last curve and pulled into the hospital grounds, the Indian mother was standing uncertainly next to the fence. She looked tired and, as there was no one else around, Marty stepped out, stretched his legs, and walked over to the woman. He spoke to her in Spanish but she did not understand.

At that moment the doctor came out the back door of the clinic. The mother took the child off her back. The baby was no longer hot; but she had come a long way, and she would not turn away now. The doctor took the lovingly held bundle. His glance was swift, professional, and knowing. The baby was dead; it had probably died hours before. There was no hope for the child.

The Indian mother took her sixth dead baby into her arms. Softly she cried the cry of all mothers who have had to surrender part of their own lives.

Jon leaned against the car and watched the woman rock back and forth. He felt sorrow for her, compassion, and decided that this was the same emotion Jesus must have felt for those He met. Jon remained in the background the rest of the day, but he was watching, observing.

The doctor was busy, so it had been Marty who walked on down the road and made arrangements for the mother and dead child to be flown back to their home. The Missionary Aviation Fellowship plane served a jungle station near where the woman's family lived. During the late afternoon Jon watched the plane take off and fly out over the carpeted jungle.

They stayed three days in Shell. Jon had a good time taking some of the "missionary kids" swimming in the

fairly placid river and then riding for hours on one of
their horses. He liked children and they had responded
to this handsome blond fellow. They let him borrow
their butterfly net and together they had hunted beetles,
spiders, and myriads of night-flying insects. Jon also
had helped his father with electrical jobs on the hospital
building.

The night before they left, they had supper with
Olga's father, who remembered Allison and her care for
his daughter. His second wife served them rich potato
soup with a fried egg floating majestically on top. Rice,
fried bananas and a slab of almost inedible beef were
the main portion, with a piece of delicious pineapple
completing the meal. The conversation was general
and, after talking for only a few moments about his
daughter, the old man had gone off to town.

The next morning Jon, Allison, and Marty drove
back to Quito. Before they left, Jon talked his mother
into buying a green stalk of one hundred bananas and
enough naranjillas to make him dozens of glasses of
juice.

After a day back in Quito, Jon was ready for another
trip. Allison, though, was tired and so she talked Jon
and Marty into going out to Papallacta without her.

Allison was vaguely aware of the HCJB hydroelectric story but, like most women, she wasn't overly fascinated by the technical details of the project. Most of
her knowlecge came from a program she had heard
over HCJB. It had been written by a woman, so that
was probably why she had understood its content.

> First it was a sheep shed,
> And God transformed it into radio station HCJB.

Then it was a cabbage patch,
And God transformed it into the compound of HCJB.

Then it was pastureland,
And God transformed it into the Pifo transmitter site.

And now it is a potato valley,
And God has transformed it into HCJB hydroelectric.

There are fifteen acres there in Papallacta which have
    been bulldozed, cut into, built onto, and now have a
    big concrete bowl, the reservoir.
And a silver thread of thirty-six-inch pipe, the penstock.
And a gray house catching it all, the powerhouse.

Up above it all is the Papallacta River, one of the
    headwaters of the mighty Amazon.
And the idea is to harness that river into that reservoir
    and down that pipe and through that powerhouse
    where it will pass along wires stretched for thirty-four
    rough miles to Pifo.

Then Pifo can take two million watts of power and sort
    it out accordingly for all the different HCJB lan-
    guages.

And program folks in Quito can preach and sing with
    confidence as they know their words are being flung
    into distant world corners.

When Jon and Marty came back to Quito after their
trip, it was almost midnight. Allison was asleep. Her
note on the table explained that she had spent most the
day getting Carmen out of the hospital and settled at an
aunt's house. Then she had bought baby clothes and
during the rest of the afternoon had tried to convince
the angry family to take their daughter and new grand-
daughter home.

The two men made themselves some toast and coffee

and talked for a couple of hours. Marty spoke for a long time about Ricardo. This was the first time they had discussed things like this, man to man. Marty sought Jon's advice about Marcos, and the young man promised that he would spend an afternoon with his Ecuadorian friend.

Jon finally asked his father the one question he had had on his mind during the flight down to Ecuador. Marty refrained from giving his son a stereotyped answer. In fact, he didn't give the boy any answer.

But by then Jon didn't need a verbal reply. He had seen both his parents "in action" again. He knew why they were in Quito.

# 5

# Results from Afar

The Wallop Building stands directly to the right of the main HCJB entrance gate. On the bottom floor are the offices for the Russian department, upstairs is the English correspondence division. On the ground-level porch, where the post office is located, an entire wall of mailboxes faces the parking lot.

By 9 A.M. all the mail is distributed. Shortly afterward the area is filled with staff members eagerly collecting their personal mail and departmental letters. After a word of greeting and a short visit, the area is clear again. People have gone to their offices to read their mail, family news first and then the important response from listeners.

Mail—this is really the end product of the entire radio thrust. Only a small percentage of those who listen to shortwave radio from Quito will ever write, yet the letters are vital to the ministry of HCJB. Through the letters the engineers learn if the signal strength is strong enough. Through the letters the broadcast people learn if their programming is heard. Through the letters the station learns that people are turning their lives over to the Lord Jesus Christ and that believers are being encouraged in their daily living of the Christian faith. Through the mail HCJB workers ultimately realize that their labor is not in vain.

## JAPANESE DEPARTMENT

An average of 333 letters are received each month in the Japanese department. On May 1, 1964, broadcasts in the Japanese language were started. Now two hours a day of Japanese programming are sent to Japan and Brazil.

The small Japanese farmer had struggled for many years in the hostile Brazilian jungle where he had to fight the constant encroachment of deadly vegetation upon his crops. Often his wife had been lonely for her island home and the mother she would never see again. Her husband had tried to maintain a loyal Japanese family in the midst of a Latin culture, and with his own children he succeeded fairly well. But now his grandchildren could not read Japanese and were quickly incorporating Brazilian habits into their speech and lives.

But, above all, he had tried to maintain the Buddhist faith in his family circle. Lovingly and with patience he taught his children to love and honor God. This they did. But six years ago his oldest son, his beloved firstborn, chose to follow the Christian God.

The boy had used his first earnings to buy a short-wave radio which soon became a prized possession in their home. The mother eased some of her loneliness by listening to programs in her own language. And the son? He developed the habit of listening to the Japanese programs from Quito, Ecuador.

And then a letter came to Quito. The envelope was addressed in English, but the letter was carefully written in Japanese characters.

DEAR FRIENDS:

I am sure that you will be surprised to receive a letter from a stranger like me. However, you are not a stranger to us. My son had very close contact with HCJB through the radio and correspondence for the last six years.

This is my first letter to you though, and I am writing this for the sake of my son. He went to be with your God last month after having a bad cold. He was only 27 years old. Strange enough, on the day he passed away we received your letter from Quito. In it we found a gospel tract entitled "A Journey to Heaven."

My son was having a good time with his brothers and sisters in the living room. Then he asked us to call a doctor because of his headache. When the doctor came, our boy was already in the other world. Not causing any trouble to anybody, he died in peace.

Many people who came to the funeral mentioned that they had never seen a face as peaceful as his. I have nothing to regret as a father for my son died, but his spirit lives forever.

Setting aside the letter, the Japanese department prayed for the family left without their eldest son, asking especially that they would find their peace in the living God. Closing the time of prayer, the staff went over to the studio building to once again record a program that would point the listener to Christ.

## RUSSIAN DEPARTMENT

The postmarks on the letters in the Russian department read like a map of the world: Kabul, Mongolia, Kiev, Leningrad, Teheran, Moscow, London, Sao Paulo, Alaska, Sydney. In June of 1941 the Slavic Gospel Association assumed responsibility for Russian broadcasts over HCJB. Today the station carries seven half-hour Russian gospel programs each day and nine on Sunday. The staff receives at least fifteen letters daily, and they have heard from thirteen of the fifteen Russian republics.

The letter from Anita was postmarked Buenos Aires. She wrote in Russian although she could have typed it in Spanish. The physical writing of the letter caused her much pain because she has muscular rheumatism.

JANUARY 4, 1969

DEAR RUSSIAN FRIENDS:

I am almost an invalid. I have no strength in my arms and feet. When I was younger, though, I was quite well. We were ten children. My own mother was a Christian. When she was alive she taught us about the Lord. She often told how she became a Christian as a young girl in Russia. How angry her father was! He wanted to kill her. Finally he threw her out of the house.

But she never stopped loving God. She encouraged each of us to walk with the Lord. She taught us to pray and to praise God. It is sad to tell, but when we were still very young children she died.

My father married again and three more children were born. Our homelife became very disturbed. I decided to go to work. But my father needed me and so I gave up my job and returned to our house. For a time I tried to teach my younger brothers and sisters about the

Lord, but the house was always in a state of confusion and I gave up on their religious training.

As time went by I developed horrible fears. They were like heavy chains about my mind. They never left me. Then came the most terrible blow of all. I had been under a doctor's care. I thought it was a passing illness. It wasn't. When he told me that I could never marry and that I would never be well, I decided to kill myself.

I first had to break off my relationship with my boy-friend. Then I set about making plans for my death. Each night I would decide to undertake this final act.

I could not do it for my mother's words kept coming to me: "Where will you spend eternity?" My body remained on earth but my soul was living in hell.

Nothing could reach me, or so it seemed. At that time I began listening to the Word of God in the Russian language coming to me from Ecuador. I was touched. It seemed that the speaker knew all about my personal life. This scared me.

I opened my Russian Bible and read the words, "Heaven and earth shall pass away, but my Word shall not pass away." I turned to God who has greatly helped me.

LOVINGLY,
ANITA

Anita continues to write to Box 691. She has started children's classes in her home, and the doctor has started a new medical treatment for her. Her letters are filled with the joy of the Lord.

## GERMAN DEPARTMENT

This is a letter received by the German department:

DEAR FRIENDS:
We are writing for the following reason. Our son

disappeared on November 16. Because all our efforts to find him have been unsuccessful until now, we would like to ask you to announce his disappearance on your German programs. Perhaps one of your listeners has seen or heard of him. His name is Carl, he is 19 years old and 6 feet tall.

On Sunday morning, November 16, he left as usual with his bicycle, but did not return. The bike was found at the main bus depot. No one knew in which direction he may have gone.

He did not take any extra clothing. However, he did have his watch, his papers, money, a knife and some maps of Brazil, Paraguay, Bolivia, Peru, Ecuador, Colombia, and Venezuela.

Again we ask, could you please announce this in your broadcasts?

The announcement was made regarding the disappearance of Carl on two programs. Besides this, the department wrote to the parents, pointing them to Christ. Letter number two arrived:

MARCH 30

DEAR GERMAN FRIENDS:

Thank you for your letter, and that you have prayed for me that I might come to the assurance of salvation. I would like to share with you that I have decided to follow Christ. I am now His child.

Not only have I accepted Christ, but we have all accepted Him. I have confessed my sins to the Lord and have the assurance that He has forgiven me and that I am a child of God. I have deep peace in my heart now.

Thank you for what you have done. We have heard nothing yet from our oldest son.

Because of your announcements on HCJB, we hope to see him again, if not here, then in glory.

A THANKFUL MOTHER.

The next letter came from the daughter in the house. She wrote:

> I would like to share with you the news that about a month ago my parents received two letters from my lost brother. He is in deep inner and outward distress. He has given us no address. I will copy his letters for you, so that you can better understand the situation he is in and will continue to pray for him.

DEAR PARENTS:
Because you have taught me nothing, I am now lost. I was in the town of P for half a year and am now in Brazil. My situation is becoming more and more hopeless. If you do not pray for me, I will never come home, nor get to heaven.

CARL

DEAR PARENTS:
I would like to come home, because it does seem to be right. What you listen to on the radio all the time, I too am listening to. I have started to read the Bible, but do not understand anything I have read. I do not have money in order to come.

CARL

After receiving this letter from their son, the family went to their pastor, who immediately wrote to a friend of his living in the Brazilian town from which Carl had written. He enclosed a picture of the boy.

The friend, a Brazilian pastor, wrote back at once to the worried family, telling them that he had seen their son sitting in front of his church, and on one occasion had spoken to him. But after that encounter he had not seen him again.

After receiving the letter with the photo, the pastor did not know where to look for Carl; but, by chance, he met him in the city shortly afterward. The young man told the pastor that he had practically no money, and that he spent the nights in various hiding places. The pastor gave him some money, and Carl bought a bus ticket to his home.

But instead of completing the trip, he got off in a town hundreds of miles from his intended destination. From that strange town he wrote to his father, telling him that he did not have enough money to come home and that he had no work. He did not give an address.

The letter was dated September 17. When the family received it on October 3, the father immediately decided to go and find his son.

Of course, the man had no way of knowing whether his son was still in the town from which he had sent the letter, but he left that same afternoon for the strange city. He supposed he was going to a small town but, to his surprise, found that it was a very large city.

His problem now was to locate Carl. All day and during the evening he went up and down the streets, looking for his son. In addition, he enlisted the help of the local radio station and the police. He had a photo of the boy with him, but nobody recognized him.

Days passed. All searching proved unsuccessful and the father was about to give up hope. Early one morning before breakfast he went out onto the street again after praying fervently that the Lord would help him find his son. Suddenly he saw a young man across the street. Didn't that look like his boy? He called his name and the young man stopped. It was he! Carl was much thinner and looked as though he had suffered from hunger. The same day they boarded a bus together.

OCTOBER 30

DEAR HCJB GERMAN DEPARTMENT:

How happy we all are. But Carl still needs your prayers in order that he too might find Jesus. We would like to thank you for your faithfulness in prayer. Let us thank Him together, that He has answered prayer.

A GRATEFUL FAMILY

The German language was first broadcast over HCJB in 1941 by a German refugee. In 1953 the Mennonite Brethren Mission Board agreed to provide HCJB with a German department. Since 1968, the department has received approximately nine hundred letters a month, and today there are six daily German programs.

## QUECHUA DEPARTMENT

In the highlands of Ecuador, Bolivia, and Peru live seven to ten million Quechua Indians. Forty-eight percent of Ecuador's population are Quechua. Though they were cruelly treated by the Spanish conquistadores, both their culture and their language have survived. Today they constitute a culture within a culture in South America.

The mountain Quechuas live in isolated villages high in the Andes. Because they are scattered and living far from cities and urban areas, reaching them with the gospel of Christ has been a difficult task. But there are Christian believers among the Quechuas. José Juan is one. Out of a heart filled with God's love, he wrote one day:

## Creation

Look at all that was created by our God,
All the beauties and the wonders of the earth.
He commanded that the plant grow from the sod,
To the sun and moon up in the sky gave birth.
   God created man, took him from the ground,
   Molded him like clay, breathed into his soul.
God put man and woman in a garden,
He would come and visit them along the way.
They lived content together there in Eden,
While they obeyed God's words each and every day.
   God created man, walked with him each day.
   Man sinned against God, then he had to pay.
One day sin and trouble came upon the two,
Satan tempted them and brought on sorrow.
They did the things that God had told them not to do,
God said they then from the garden had to go.
   God created man, walked with him each day.
   Man sinned against God, but God's own Son did pay.

                    English words by PAT LARSON

Quechua broadcasts were begun in 1932 and today HCJB beams eight hours a week of programming to Ecuador, Peru, and Bolivia. There are agricultural, public health, world and local news programs in addition to regular gospel programs. But since few Quechuas can write, the letter response is very slight.

## SPANISH DEPARTMENT

It was a dark, rainy morning, a sad Ecuadorian day. The lady working in her tiny kitchen was a Christian believer who lived about five hours from Quito in an isolated mountain village. It was a quiet settlement where nothing of great import ever occurred.

The main highway was miles away and the days were rarely interrupted by anybody or anything. That is why Maria was surprised when she heard the report of guns and the snarling of dogs. Her active imagination immediately pictured a dangerous criminal being chased into the isolated mountains.

She had started walking toward the door to investigate the unusual activity when she remembered her program, "Femenidades" from radio station HCJB, was on. This daily contact with Christians was her delight, and even the thought of a mysterious adventure could not keep her from turning on her radio and sitting down to listen.

When the program was finished, she began to do some mending, her thoughts still on the radio program. She did not hear the man until he stood behind her chair. He was bleeding from a head wound and his appearance was one of tired desperation.

Maria sat very still and, although she was afraid, she realized that she must offer him some kind of Christian help. Without doubt, this was the man who had brought the police into the mountains.

"Please, help me," he pleaded.

"Of course I will," she answered. "Come into the bedroom and let me wash your wounds."

He lay on her bed and sat up only to drink a cup of warm milk. Soon he was asleep and she ran to her neighbor's house. After a few hours, she decided to return home, where she found the stranger sitting up. He quickly responded to her request for information.

"A week ago Tuesday I got into an argument with a

friend of mine. We began to push and shove one another, and when he hit me in the face I lost my temper and shoved him with all my might. He stumbled backward and then fell into the ditch. His head hit some metal scraps and he died immediately.

"Everyone began to shout at me, calling me a murderer. I was greatly afraid. I have been running ever since and this morning the police almost caught me. Could I not ask of you a place of safe dwelling? Let me stay until I know which road I should travel."

Maria's kind heart could not refuse the man a place of refuge. He slept that night in her warm kitchen.

The following day he listened with interest to the Spanish broadcasts from HCJB. In the afternoon he helped Maria with the chores on her small farm. As the days passed, her "guest" became deeply interested in the Christian message and would often discuss what he had heard over the air. He was an industrious man, willing to work, and he spent his time helping the entire village.

After many weeks he felt strong enough to travel and one morning told his new friends, "Now I must go. Thank you for taking pity on me. My body has been healed here in your tiny village. But, as you know from our talks, something more wonderful has happened. My spirit has been healed by the Lord Jesus Christ. He has bound up my wounds and forgiven me all my sins."

With one accord the town asked the man to stay. Maria and others offered to give him a tiny piece of their meager land and, without hesitation, the fugitive accepted their offers. He built a small house and dedicated it to the Lord. It became the village church.

He grew vegetables and sold them in the market,

saving his money so he could buy a radio. Often he walked into town and brought back books about the Christian life.

One day he brought a box of Bibles to the village and presented them to all who wished to read God's Word. After this loving act, Maria decided that she would make the long bus trip to Quito. She wanted to talk with somebody at radio station HCJB.

When she walked into the office of the Ecuadorian missionary who writes "Femenidades," she was all smiles.

"I have come many miles to tell you the miracle God has performed. He has sent to us a true pastor, a man greatly changed because God's Spirit now lives in his heart. This man listens always to the programs of HCJB and then teaches us all that he has learned.

"God has paid the debt for this man's sins. Now our pastor has a debt to pay to society. We pray that soon God will give him strength to go back to his town. We know God will walk the road with him."

Maria was a fat woman, used to much hard work. As an act of love, she took the missionary's hand, saying, "I have come all this way to tell you of how God brought to our village a pastor and a church. Thank you."

Spanish was the language first used over radio station HCJB. There were few radios in Ecuador when HCJB made its first broadcast on Christmas Day, 1931. However, the vision of what radio would become was strong and, as the receivers increased countrywide and worldwide, so did the Spanish broadcasts.

For many years thousands of pretuned radios were distributed throughout Ecuador by HCJB's Radio

Circle. However, with the advent of the transistor and the ready availability of the low-cost Japanese radios, it became no longer necessary for the station to make pretuned radios. Almost everyone in Ecuador owns at least one radio. Radios, like bicycles and wrist watches, have become the status symbols of increasing affluence.

From HCJB's strategic location in Ecuador, it is possible to serve virtually all the countries of Central and South America with Spanish broadcasts. Special programs in Spanish are also beamed to Spain.

The Bible Institute of the Air carries on an extensive training program based largely on contacts made through radio broadcasts. Enrollment has grown from two thousand in 1949 to almost ten times that number of students today. Students from more than twenty countries are enrolled in courses ranging from beginner Bible studies to advanced seminary-level work.

## ENGLISH DEPARTMENT

"Leslie," said the postmaster, "it looks like you're making friends around the world." He handed the young engineer two letters.

"It's true," replied Leslie, quickly placing the envelopes in his pocket. "Aren't I in here twice a week to get my mail? And doesn't my mail come from many different places? There are other countries in the world besides our India, and I'm anxious to know them all."

"Youth—that's what it is—youth," sighed the postmaster of Jabalpur. Then he smiled. He liked Leslie and was pleased that the twenty-five-year-old bachelor was spending his time in seeking new ideas and new friends. He knew that the boy listened every evening to his shortwave radio. In fact, he'd been in the store when Leslie bought his three yards of copper-wire net for his indoor aerial arrangement.

"Well, son, I'll see you in a couple of days. Go on home and read your letters from Ecuador and Czechoslovakia."

Leslie turned and, with a wave of his fine brown hand, disappeared down the worn steps.

He saved his mail for suppertime. He did not like to eat alone and therefore looked forward to having his letters for company. Tonight, though, he was anxious to read his letter from Radio Prague, so he opened it the minute he sat down at the table. Quickly scanning the page, he knew immediately that he had won!

There it was. A six-year scholarship to study radio engineering in Czechoslovakia! He was thrilled. He wanted to share his good news and excitement and thought of phoning his friend at the post office.

But then he remembered his second letter and turned his attention to it. It was from Quito, Ecuador. Leslie was a DX-er and was monitoring about fifteen radio stations. When he first started listening to HCJB, he had been disappointed in the reception. But at the time India was not a target area, so Leslie had been picking up the fringes of a signal beamed to Australia and New Zealand. The quality of the reception hadn't discouraged him, however, and he had become a regular listener.

It always surprised him to think that a large radio station would take the time to correspond personally with any listener who wrote. But here it was, another two-page letter. When he finished reading it he decided to let them know about his good fortune.

All of you will be happy to know that I won first prize from Radio Prague's "Scholarship Contest" to study radio engineering in Czechoslovakia. I expect to leave by the end of this year at the latest. So I will be able to listen to HCJB in that country, as no doubt you do beam your transmissions to that part of the world. But of course that depends if a radio is available for me there. However, I shall be glad to let you know by and by.

And he did write again as he had promised:

Yes, I am in Czechoslovakia. I arrived here on October 28th. After a few days in lovely Prague I am now in Senec, which is a charming little town in the eastern region of this country. I'll be here for a year studying the Slovak language. I can not start to study the engineering course until completion of my language work. This language is tough, especially the grammar.

Czechoslovakia is a beautiful and classical country. The people are the most friendly I have ever known. They are very courteous and in the village here they are very simple and always ready to give a helping hand to a stranger. They are a contented people and all work very hard, the very old and young alike. What happened to them during the past few months [Russia entered the country and replaced the liberal leaders with those more in line with Russian policy], they have taken with a shrug and they try not to cry. To them, what's done cannot be undone. They are very wise.

I am so sorry I cannot listen to HCJB here as I do not have a radio of my own. Being a keen SWL, I miss it very, very much.

When Leslie received his next letter from Quito, he read these words:

We have read of the Russian invasion. In these troublesome days, I'm glad that I'm a Christian. There is no peace in the world, but I am happy for peace of heart which comes from knowing Christ Jesus.

The young man was having a difficult time with the language and was becoming very discouraged. Many of his new friends encouraged him to learn the language by spending some time in the pubs and beer halls. But he was an absolute teetotaler and really not overly gregarious, so he had to look for some other means of picking up the language. He wrote again to HCJB, although he had not heard the station for over a year. His letter was warm and filled with news.

Being too busy with the Slovak language, I really don't have time to listen to World News on the student radio here. So I guess it's good in a way that I do not have a radio. I'll just have to get used to being without one. . . .

You, of course, know about the Czech students committing suicide by burning themselves in protest against Russian occupation. This of course is very foolish, serving no worthy cause, but simply giving rise to more complications and sorrow.

As you know, this country is a Catholic one, but I was surprised to observe that in Prague the Czech youth do not attend church services. I was given to understand that they have turned atheists. This in turn is due to their level of education and the condition of the world.

However, there is real religious freedom and it is guaranteed by the constitution. I note that this freedom is everywhere respected. Churches are open and are scenes of regular services.

He concluded his letter:

> Thank you for your word about Christian principles.
> It was appreciated. I hope and pray the day will come
> when all Christians will be united. As it is, we Chris-
> tians are subjected to amusement, scoffing and laughter
> from non-Christians. Very often they tell me: "A house
> divided against itself can never stand."

A Christmas card came from Leslie this year but no
word of greeting. The English staff recognizes that
there is a great battle going on for the minds of men.
For many, the battle language is English, today's uni-
versal language. Like Greek of old, it has become the
modern missionary tongue. One out of every six people
in the world understands English. Half of the world's
newspapers and scientific journals are published in this
language.

Each year 16,000 letters cross the desks of those
working in the English correspondence department.
Communicating the truth to these and thousands of
others who never write is a tremendous responsibility.
To cross the gulf from sender to receiver, the broadcast
must speak the language of the listener in words and
concepts he can understand. HCJB is attempting to do
just that.

## SWEDISH DEPARTMENT

HCJB has had Swedish programs since 1937. Today
a daily half-hour program is transmitted at three
different hours for reception throughout the world.
About 3,500 letters are received each year.

A thirty-eight-year old seaman picked up HCJB while sailing in the Pacific Ocean, fifteen degrees south of the equator in 1966. He had been a shortwave listener for some years. When he happened to tune in the Swedish broadcast, the announcer was telling about a rich man storing up more and more for the future. The seaman thought that this was a perfect picture of his own life, except that he wasn't exactly rich! As he stood on the ship's deck beneath the star-filled night, he felt very small indeed. He wrote the Swedish department and thanked them for sending a word from God.

A year later in 1967 the sailor was spending his spare hours with shortwave radio. He told HCJB that the things which used to give him a thrill no longer attracted him. He was starting to sense an inner peace and found that he was enjoying his job more and more.

Having changed jobs, in 1969 the sailor was living in southern Sweden. He happily received a New Testament and promised to read it through. Impressed by the story of a listener who found life in God after listening to the radio programs for seventeen years, he requested the staff to pray that he too would find Christ.

During one of the long winter nights of 1970, the former seaman met his God. While listening to the broadcast he found himself at a crossroad in his heart and mind and decided to commit his life to Jesus Christ. Looking back on his life, he realized that he could have become a Christian years before. He went to Sunday school, but no one in his family was a Christian. Once he had asked his parents about Christ coming to live in a boy's life; they assured him that this was a matter people didn't talk about, so he kept his need buried.

Soon life took him far away from Christian influences and he literally sailed around the world. Life was rough and often the circumstances were grim, but God prevented him from ever committing a crime.

Today he writes: "I thank God for HCJB. They have brought new life in Christ to me. I feel it! I know it is mine and I live it every day."

Most of the Swedish listeners come from Sweden, but many write from Norway, Denmark, and parts of Finland. Many of them are seamen filling lonely hours with shortwave programs from HCJB.

## PORTUGUESE DEPARTMENT

In the beginning Hilda hated living in the jungles. She was from Sao Paulo and considered herself a cultured Brazilian girl. But when she married Carlos she had to leave the modern and throbbing city and move to a rubber plantation thousands of miles from the security of her childhood. She became lonely, but, more than that, she felt afraid. The heat of the lowlands oppressed her, and the strange animals and their constant noises frightened her.

But fortunately Carlos was a kind man, and he patiently helped her to understand the strange surroundings. She came to find beauty in the equatorial forest, and by the time her three babies had been born she was very much at home.

Carlos soon built a lovely home on a hill overlooking the brown river. Spreading out behind their houses were dozens of tents in which Carlos' employees lived. They too brought their families with them, and the tiny settlement took on the flavor of a pioneer village. Everyone contributed money for a school-teacher, so the children grew up receiving a good Brazilian education as well as learning to respect the jungle and having countless exotic pets.

However, both Hilda and Carlos wanted more for their children, so they began reading to them from the Bible. They longed for the children to know God and desired that a church be built on the rubber plantation. Over the years the dream of an actual church building was never realized, but the more important longing was fulfilled: their children came to know God.

Once a month Carlos, Hilda, and their three children made a harrowing journey to the nearest town. Three days had to be spent on the water before the small river town was reached, but even when the children were babies, their parents took them along. They felt it was important for the children to grow up knowing that there was more beyond the dreamlike existence at the site of their home.

On one of their first trips into town, Carlos bought a shortwave radio. Through the years it kept the family in touch with world events, entertained them, and finally, in 1964, brought them their first Portuguese church service. The program came from Quito, Ecuador.

On their very next trip they carried with them a letter addressed to HCJB. Hilda began the habit of writing a monthly greeting. Her most recent letter reads like that of a dear old friend, but a friend none of the missionaries has ever met.

MY DEAREST FRIENDS AT HCJB:
Thank you so much for all the wonderful programs you are sending to us here in Brazil. And thanks also for

all the letters and tracts you mail to us. You don't know
how much each little thing from you means to us. I don't
know if you realize where we live, but I want to tell it to
you. Then you might understand more fully why your
programs and friendship are so precious to my husband,
children, and myself.

We are a happy family of five; my husband and I have
been married for twenty years. Our three children, a girl
and two boys, are wonderful and we thank the Lord for
the precious salvation that He has given each of us. We
live here, at the border of Bolivia. The nearest town
takes us three days to reach. We have to travel by a
little motor boat to get there. We make the trip to this
town once a month. We always go together, the whole
family. We do our shopping, get our mail and try to be in
town for the Sunday service at our church.

Since we started listening years ago, we never miss
your programs. Of course when we are in town we listen
to you there. And every month we find a letter from you
waiting for us at the post office. We always send you a
letter right back. Well, I tell you all this because I want
you to know how we live in this part of Brazil. You may
wonder why we live so far from town. My husband is
the supervisor of 200 men that are working on a rubber
plantation. We are trying to establish a little church
here, in the jungle. Most of our workers have transistor
radios and from almost all of their tents we can hear you
preaching at 9 P.M. every night.

I have so much more to tell you, but I will wait for
the next time. And let me finish by asking you, "Do you
understand now why we love you and your Portuguese
Department so much?"

HILDA, CARLOS AND ALL

P.S. Please send us some tracts for distribution among
the unbelievers that work for us.

In order to reach the largest country of South America with a positive gospel message, HCJB sought out Brazilian couples to initiate a Portuguese ministry. Now three half-hour programs are released daily to the giant country lying to the east of Ecuador. Over 10,000 letters a year give evidence to the fact that countless Brazilians are listening to shortwave radio.

# 6

# Resolve: New and Renewed

Though our stirring speeches speed round the world on
our radio and TV and we have not love we are like
blaring brass and crashing machinery.

"Anything good on television?" Jon had settled himself on the brown chair and stretched his long legs
across the footstool. He didn't glance up as he asked
his father about the evening television schedule because he was absorbed in some family pictures that
Allison had brought out. It was his last night home.

"At 9 P.M. Tom Jones is on channel eight. It's in
English." Marty briefly noted the TV announcements
in the paper.

Allison was sitting next to him on the sofa, the soft
yellow lamp spreading light over the photographs in her
lap. She wanted to forget that this was Jon's last night.
She wished she could stand up and physically hold
back the passing of the hours. In her mind she could
visualize herself, back tightly pressed against time, pre-
venting it from continuing its terrible, relentless, nev-
er-stopping march.

But it wasn't time that was Allison's real enemy. Her

foe was separation. She had never been able to reconcile herself to being separated from those she loved.

Allison had grown up in a rural community where both the elementary and high schools shared the same tree-splashed acre. The county hospital where she trained was on the edge of town, and her life, friends, church, work, and school were contained in one small, secure geographical area.

When she and Marty had left for Ecuador, Allison's emotion had been one of almost unbearable physical pain. It was as if she were being torn from the womb. In her own mind the experience of leaving everyone and everything that was safe and familiar was like having a limb amputated without anesthesia. She often argued with herself that she was overdramatizing the situation, but she never won the argument; her feelings were too real, too intense.

At first she didn't share her reaction about leaving home with anyone else except Marty. Although he did not fully understand her sense of loss, he did sympathize with her. For a long time she felt guilty, as if her loneliness were something that God would disapprove of, and she would alternately pray and worry about her attitude.

There were times when she thought she had buried the lingering sadness. But then her sister married, her brother's wife had twin sons, and her father became ill. Each experience reminded her once again that she was far, far from home, and she would find herself back fighting the same old battle.

One day Allison finally realized that it was a battle she was destined never to win. She would always feel, to some degree, the pain of separation. And so she accepted it as one accepts a physical handicap. She looked at it, acknowledged its presence, and determined that it would not ruin her life with Marty. It would not taint their stay in Ecuador.

Her resolve had remained constant, although at times shaken. When her father died, Allison was almost overcome with the feeling of loss and the gulf which stretched between her and her family.

*Separation.* Slowly she began to realize that God was an understanding presence during her difficult moments. Hadn't Jesus Christ Himself been separated from His eternal home? Did He long for all He left behind when He came to earth to live with people?

The assurance that God understood her feelings was the basis of her stability when Jon and his brother left to go to college in the United States. But Allison knew her enemy well, and she knew it was in the room this evening. She leaned over toward Marty and let her head rest on his shoulder.

*Well, Lord, You know that old feeling is coming back.*

*I dread tomorrow morning when Jon will leave.*

*I don't want him to go.*

*But it would be ridiculous for him to stay with us forever. Silly thought.*

*Yet my heart hurts. You know that, don't You?*

*Well, I'm just telling You how I feel.*

*Now, could You help me out, please? Put this dread in the back of the bottom drawer in the dresser.*

*Thank you.*

Jon set the pictures aside and asked again about television. "Let's see what HCJB's channel 4 has to offer," he commented as he reached across the footstool and turned on the portable set.

It was a surprise to everyone in the room when the

family dentist came into view. There he sat, facing the cameras and looking very much at home in the Western setting of the television program. The backdrop had been painted to resemble a North American prairie scene from the 1800s. Apparently the Ecuadorian community had seen enough United States cowboy movies to appreciate the scenery.

The pioneers who flanked the guest were having a good time visiting with the doctor. A few minutes of listening to the Spanish conversation revealed to the viewers that Dr. Lopez had adjusted himself to the theme of the program and was fitting his Christian testimony into the program format.

Jon looked at his father and smiled. He remembered the Saturday morning five years ago when they had gone to visit Dr. Lopez in his home.

The entire family had driven out to keep the appointment with Dr. Lopez. They had been invited for morning coffee but were unaware of the reason behind the invitation. It was one of those experiences that had puzzled Jon. But now that he was hearing the man on television he had a better appreciation of the visit.

Finding the doctor's home had been no problem. He lived directly across from the entrance to the airport, the third house on the left. The entire Lopez family was in the living room. Their rushed greetings were uncustomarily short for a Latin family, but apparently the doctor had something on his mind.

"I invited you here for a reason. I want to know about your religion." Dr. Lopez spoke directly to Marty. "We've been friends for years, Marty. How long have I been your dentist?"

He didn't wait for a reply, but rushed on. "But I've never paid much attention to your religious belief. You thought your way and I thought mine. But this has changed everything."

With a dramatic sweep of his arm he indicated what he meant by "this." It was a large console television set which occupied the place of honor against the brick wall.

"When we first bought the set we avoided HCJB. I didn't want to be bothered with religious programs. But people would come into my office and ask if I'd seen the news on HCJB. I'd say no. Then another patient would ask if I'd watched the comedy series on HCJB. I'd say no. Even the children in the office would quiz me about my viewing habits. Finally my wife began watching the cooking program, and when she and my daughter used some of the recipes, we were all grateful to HCJB."

Senora Lopez laughed and, looking at her husband, she continued the explanation.

"At first we only turned to HCJB for the dramatic series. Then one night we watched the closing program."

The dentist was too involved with his thoughts to let his wife take the lead, and he interrupted her.

"You know the program, Marty, those last few minutes when you have a closing thought. Well, that first night we heard the man give a Bible verse. We thought it was interesting. The next night I decided to look up the verse in our own Bible. Just wanted to see if my Bible and your announcer agreed. They did. And since then we have ended every day with HCJB-TV."

It was then that Marty saw the Bible on top of the TV set. His glance was noted by Dr. Lopez.

"Yes, we look up the verse each evening. We want to know God in the same way you do, Marty. Help us to understand what the Bible is telling us about Jesus Christ."

Everyone in the room focused his attention on Marty. Jon was amazed that this man and his family would be so frank about what they wanted to know, and Allison was amazed at the apparent change in the dentist's attitude toward God's truth. Television had quietly and inoffensively prepared this family to be receptive to God's Word.

* * *

Television equipment from a bankrupt station lay discarded on the scrap pile, ready for melting down. It was 1955 and a General Electric technician-engineer looked over the junk. He felt he could take all the scrapped material and build a television transmitter to be used for missionary broadcasting. When General Electric accepted his offer of $200.00 for the pile of metal, he happily trucked home the beginnings of HCJB's television transmitter.

Not until 1959 did the engineer and his equipment arrive in Quito. They came after the Newspaper Union of Ecuador had invited HCJB to give Ecuadorians a demonstration of television at that year's National Fair. A hectic period began for everyone working in this new media. Less time was available for the preparation and testing of the equipment than would have been ideal. There were temporary installations, cramped quarters in studio and control room, and lack of experience in many areas. But in August the first official HCJB-TV program was televised.

Television was a novelty and, as such, was eagerly received by those at the fair. It arrested the public's attention just as it had done around the world when it was first shown.

In 1961 the Ecuadorean government granted HCJB a license to operate the world's first missionary television station.

As Allison continued to listen to Marty's explanation to the dentist and his family, she recalled with clarity the ups and downs of HCJB-TV, including the many controversial discussions which had taken place within the mission society concerning its television policy. It seemed to Allison that this particular entertainment medium would always stir up some type of debate. It was in the very nature of the media, in the very nature of man.

But for Dr. Lopez and his family, the benefits of TV were all positive, and that Saturday morning they committed themselves to follow Jesus Christ.

As Jon watched the conclusion of the television program, he realized that the doctor's decision had not been some momentary whim. The man had chosen to live for Jesus Christ and was now speaking of this choice to his fellow Ecuadorians.

Jon turned off the receiver and turned to face his parents. He wanted them to know that he was glad he had been able to come to Quito for these ten days. After he shared his feelings with them, they talked about his future college work. His parents encouraged him to continue with his Latin American studies and then talked with him about a lot of other things during that last night home. All three left unsaid some things which didn't need to be verbalized.

Jon stored away impressions of his brief visit in his memory bank. Soon he would take them out, sort them, digest them, and come to his own conclusions about his parents' life direction and his own in relation to theirs. He knew he wouldn't walk the same job path his father had, and he sensed that he wouldn't be a missionary. But he did make up his mind to come to know God in a manner similar to his father's. He had caught a glimpse of the important element, the motivating force, the dominant characteristic in the lives of both Marty and Allison, and he liked what he saw.

The giant orange jet lifted off the sun-heated Ecuadorian airstrip. Marty and Allison shaded their eyes against the equatorial brightness, watched the great machine clear the fence, climb steadily into the blue Andean sky, and then bank out over the city for the turn toward the north. Within minutes the plane and their son were gone from sight.

Leaning back in his seat, Jon flew into his future.

> Though our jet engines roar ever faster over continents and oceans,
> Though we plumb the depths of the sea and tread the face of the moon or Mars,
> Though we perform heart transplants and discover new miracle drugs,
> Though we solve all problems and mysteries so that even our computers break down with the weight of our answers,
> Though we do all these things, and have not love, we are nothing.

The young man relaxed. He knew his parents had something — something of value — something he too could appropriate.

# Appendix A

## Highlights in the History of HCJB

1930 Permit for HCJB was obtained by means of a special decree of the president of Ecuador, confirmed by a vote of Congress.

1931 December 25 was the inaugural day for HCJB. The first program was broadcast from HCJB over a 250-watt transmitter in the afternoon.

1934 The Radio Circle was inaugurated.

1935 A new RCA transmitter which operated on 73 meters was added, making it possible for not only Ecuador to hear but also the neighboring republics.

1937 HCJB became a bilingual station as English programs were added to Spanish.

1938 Various gospel broadcasters in the United States began to sponsor their programs on HCJB.

1939 The "Voice of the Andes" moved from its original site to a location at the northern city limits of Quito.

1940 On Easter Sunday, the new 10,000-watt transmitter was inaugurated by the president of Ecuador. This sent HCJB's signal around the world.

1941 The number of languages used at HCJB was increased to five.

1942 The first United States office of WRMF, Inc. opened in New York City.

1943 Four new languages were added to the broadcasting schedule, making a total of nine languages.

1945 A fifth transmitter operating on 19 meters was added.

1947 The Bible Institute of the Air was organized. WRMF, Inc. became a corporation in Ecuador.

1948 On January 17, the Ecuadorian government extended the contract for the Pioneer Missionary Broadcaster to 1980. Also, the president of Ecuador conferred a high honor upon HCJB, namely membership in the National Order of Merit.

1949 The Medical Department of HCJB was inaugurated, along with the work of the Indian Hostel Clinic. Rural Medical Missions began.

1950 The Second Evangelical Church of Quito was dedicated. Six huge transformers arrived in Quito as the first installment of the "Advance Program."

1951 Forty-five acres of land were purchased for the new transmitter site, located 15 miles east of Quito in Pifo.

1952 The broadcasting schedule was extended, giving a 21-hour-a-day ministry. New property for the North American headquarters was acquired in Talcottville, Connecticut.

1953 HCJB's transmitters were moved to the new Pifo property and placed in operation. The LAM and WRMF, Inc. began to operate HOXO in Panama.

1955 The Rimmer Memorial Hospital, the first evangelical hospital in Ecuador, opened. The Palmer School of Nursing received its first group of students.

1956 The new 50,000-watt transmitter was completed and on the air. HCJB radio services and personnel actively helped in the emergency connected with the Auca incident.

1957 The first class of auxiliary nurses graduated from Palmer School of Nursing.

1958 The Epp Memorial Hospital in Shell Mera opened to serve Ecuador's eastern jungle region.

1959 The National Fair in Quito featured a nightly HCJB telecast in accordance with a provisional permit granted. HCJB-TV thus became the first missionary TV, and the first TV in Ecuador.

1960 The new diesel generator, which weighs ten and a half tons and can produce 300,000 watts of power, was installed in Pifo.

1961 On May 18, HCJB was granted a full license to operate the pioneer missionary television station, HCJB-TV.

1962 The hydroelectric plant arrived, and this great project's construction was begun.

1963 WRMF, Inc. began to sponsor Radio Cometa in Sao Paulo, Brazil, and provided four programs daily on this commercial station serving five million people.

1964 The WRMF, Inc. made a joint statement with Back to the Bible Broadcast, announcing the transfer of Back to the Bible's French and Italian ministries to WRMF.

1965 April 10 was the inauguration of the hydroelectric plant, making 2000 kilowatts of power available for future expansion.

1967 A new Spanish hymnbook for Latin America was published.

1968 In May, a TV repeater station opened in Ambato.

1969 The Jones Television Center was inaugurated.

1970 A parade through Quito climaxed Evangelism in Depth.

1971 HCJB began to broadcast with half a million watts of power.

# Appendix B

## Fourteen Strategic Languages Broadcasted by HCJB

| LANGUAGE | TARGET AREA |
| --- | --- |
| Danish | Europe |
| English | Europe, India, North American and Caribbean, South Pacific |
| French | Europe, South Pacific |
| German | Europe, North and South America |
| Hungarian | Europe |
| Japanese | Japan, South America |
| Norwegian | Europe |
| Polish | Poland |
| Portuguese | Brazil |
| Quechua | South America |
| Romanian | Europe |
| Russian | Europe, Far East and South Pacific, North and South America, Siberia |
| Spanish | Europe, the Americas |
| Swedish | Europe |